To Kathleen and Jim,
Thank for your long friendship to the Garden.
All best, Frank Robinson

Lewis Ginter Botanical Garden

25 YEARS AND GROWING

Kathleen and Jim,
Thanks for your support of the Garden!
Lynn Kirk

Lewis Ginter Botanical Garden
25 YEARS & GROWING

Lewis Ginter Botanical Garden

25 YEARS AND GROWING

Frank L. Robinson, Editor
Lynn J. Kirk, Author

THE
DONNING COMPANY
PUBLISHERS

Cover photo credit: David Hunter Hale

Copyright © 2009 by Lewis Ginter Botanical Garden

All rights reserved, including the right to reproduce this work in any form whatsoever without permission in writing from the publisher, except for brief passages in connection with a review. For information, please write:

Lewis Ginter Botanical Garden
1800 Lakeside Avenue
Richmond, Virginia 23228-4700
(804) 262-9887
www.lewisginter.org

For the Donning Company Publishers:
Richard A. Horwege, *Senior Editor*
Stephanie Danko, *Graphic Designer*
Dennis N. Walton, *Project Director*

Library of Congress Cataloging-in-Publication Data
Kirk, Lynn J.
  Lewis Ginter Botanical Garden : 25 years and growing / Frank L. Robinson, editor ; Lynn J. Kirk, author.
    p.   cm.
    ISBN 978–1–57864–552–7 (hard cover : alk. paper)—ISBN 978–1–57864–553–4 (soft cover : alk. paper)
  1. Lewis Ginter Botanical Garden (Richmond, Va.)—Guidebooks. 2. Lewis Ginter Botanical Garden (Richmond, Va.)—Pictorial works. 3. Ginter, Lewis, 1824–1897. I. Robinson, Frank L. II. Title.
  QK73.U62L49 2009
  580.7'3755451—dc22

2009005192

Printed in the USA by Walsworth Publishing Company

Printed on Recycled Paper

CONTENTS

WELCOME   8

THE GARDEN TODAY

E. Claiborne Robins Visitors Center   10
Central Garden   13
- North Terrace
- Four Seasons Garden
- Healing Garden
- Sunken Garden

Education and Library Complex   16
- Joan Massey Conference Center
- Charles F. Gillette Education Center
- Lora M. Robins Library
- Evelyn G. Luck Garden

Conservatory   18
Rose Garden   22
Henry M. Flagler Perennial Garden   26
Asian Valley   30
- Lora and Claiborne Robins Tea House

Martha and Reed West Island Garden   34
Bloemendaal House   38
Grace Arents Garden   41

Friendship Garden, Wildside Walk, and Lace House   44
Children's Garden   48
Sydnor Lake   53
Lucy Payne Minor Memorial Garden   56
Margaret Johanna Streb Conifer Garden   57
Vienna Cobb Anderson Wildflower Meadow   58
Anne Holt Massey Greenhouses   60
Special Collections   61

THE GARDEN'S HISTORY

Lewis Ginter   64
Grace E. Arents and Bloemendaal Farm   72
Historical Timeline   78

THE GARDEN'S FUTURE

The Next Decade   82
Volunteerism and Membership   85
Garden for All Seasons   86

DESIGN TEAMS   92
BOARD OF DIRECTORS   94
STAFF   95
VOLUNTEERS   95
ACKNOWLEDGMENTS   96
ABOUT THE EDITOR AND AUTHOR   96

WELCOME!

*T*wenty-five years and growing. . . .

Whether you've visited Lewis Ginter Botanical Garden once or countless times since our earliest days, this books records for all the Garden's remarkable growth and success during its first quarter-century. It is not an exaggeration to say that the Garden has surpassed the hopes of even its most ardent supporters.

This pictorial history recognizes the legacy, generosity, and vision of so many in the philanthropic and nonprofit communities. From a mere dream that began with a bequest from Grace Arents, Lewis Ginter's niece, the Garden has grown to become one of the most outstanding botanical gardens in the United States.

This book interprets the Garden as it reveals itself to our visitors, hopefully making your experience even more memorable and meaningful. The Garden overflows with beautiful plants, fascinating collections, and year-round displays, but it also reflects the passions and interests of so many who have contributed to its development. It is this human dimension that truly enriches and deepens the exploration of its treasures. As such, the Garden is "common ground"—a place for all to enjoy the pursuits of pleasure, learning, and retreat. Whether you are young or old, a professional or novice gardener, we invite you to return often—as visitor, member, donor, or volunteer.

I thank Lynn Kirk for her initiative and effort in writing and directing the production of this history; the Roller-Bottimore Foundation for its generous support enabling us to document this remarkable, comprehensive volume; and all those in the region who have given so much of themselves in time, energy, advocacy, dedication, and financial contributions to make Lewis Ginter Botanical Garden a reality.

Lewis Ginter Botanical Garden: 25 YEARS AND GROWING

We now begin our journey through the next twenty-five years. Who knows what it holds, but we have built a strong foundation and if history can provide a window into the future, ours should be an exciting future, indeed!

Frank L. Robinson

Frank L. Robinson
Executive Director
Lewis Ginter Botanical Garden
1800 Lakeside Avenue
Richmond, Virginia 23228-4700
(804) 262-9887
www.lewisginter.org

Like a beautiful butterfly having emerged from its cocoon, Lewis Ginter Botanical Garden has magically transformed over the last twenty-five years.

THE GARDEN TODAY
E. Claiborne Robins Visitors Center
GATEWAY TO THE GARDEN

Rising gracefully upon a landscaped knoll, the Visitors Center beckons all to Lewis Ginter Botanical Garden. The building's classic Neo-Georgian architecture celebrates the history and heritage of Virginia, while its interior spaces—with soaring ceilings, natural light, and panoramic garden views—create a reception area of remarkable beauty. Designed to provide key visitor amenities, the Visitors Center encompasses twenty-three thousand square feet on two levels and houses the **Garden Shop**; the **Garden Café** and terrace; the elegant **Robins Room** for meetings and community events; **Ginter Gallery I** exhibit area; volunteer and member services; and most importantly, a welcoming introduction to the region's all-season Garden.

History: The Visitors Center opened in 1999 as the first major structure built in response to the Garden's Master Plan. As such, it established Lewis Ginter Botanical Garden in the community's consciousness. Visitation tripled to 180,000 that year, launching the Garden's popularity and growth which have continued to this day.

The Visitors Center was given in memory of E. Claiborne Robins Sr. by his wife, Lora McGlasson Robins. Mr. Robins was chief executive officer of A. H. Robins International and a prominent philanthropist in the Richmond community, most notably the University of Richmond. Mrs. Robins, who was a founding member of the Garden's Board of Directors in 1984, was instrumental in establishing the building's aesthetic standards, which reflect the color, beauty, and diversity of nature.

Lewis Ginter Botanical Garden: 25 YEARS AND GROWING

The Robins Room was given by Mr. and Mrs. E. Claiborne Robins Jr., and the administrative offices by Troutman Sanders LLP. Additional funding also was provided by the Cabell Foundation, Universal Corporation, and Philip Morris USA.

In 2006, Robert E. Anderson III and family donated the Polly Anderson Terrace, adjoining the Garden Shop, in tribute to her co-founding and dedication to the gift shop and its continued success.

Central Garden

SERIES OF THEMED GARDEN ROOMS

Exiting the Visitors Center, the Central Garden unfolds in a visual progression of four intriguing garden rooms. Each features a framed, intimate space with classical thematic design, as well as fascinating plants, garden ornaments, and interpretive signage. Bordered by the Visitors Center, Conservatory, and Education and Library Complex, the Central Garden visually and physically links these key buildings.

North Terrace: In this first garden space, sounds of splashing water, mingled garden fragrances, and dramatic views transition guests from worldly distractions to tranquil garden environs. A central fountain faced with glazed-tile magnolia leaves welcomes visitors to the North Terrace Garden and courtyard.

Four Seasons Garden: Enter the next garden room for a glimpse of classical, early twentieth-century Arts and Crafts design. The Four Seasons Garden employs fine craftsmanship, as well as indigenous stone and recycled building materials. A cobbled walk slows the visitor's pace for enjoyment of the whimsical frog fountain and the mythical Green Man who represents the connection between man and nature. This garden's focus—year-round bloom and color—is demonstrated by plants that offer attractive form, color, and character even during winter dormancy. Stone walls capture solar heat during spring and autumn, thereby extending the garden's overall blooming season.

Arbor Garden: During spring and summer, the Arbor Garden blossoms to life. Its succession of arched trellises bestows beauty and invites an intimate exploration amid weeping Japanese cherries and seasonal vines. Come winter, GardenFest lighting illumines the arbors with the glitter of holiday splendor.

Healing Garden: The Healing Garden reflects the centuries-old use of plants for medicine and healing. To the west is a small-scale garden whose size and symmetry are reminiscent of a medieval cloister garden. It is designed as a place for spiritual healing through contemplation, meditation, and reflection.

Opposite is a complementing garden fashioned in an ellipse, accented by an oversized granite mortar and pestle that symbolize plants' pharmacological significance. The inspiration for this garden is the 1545 Renaissance Garden in Padua, Italy.

Sunken Garden: Step down into the Sunken Garden and experience the landscape of second-century Rome, when urban gardens were strategically located at lower elevations to benefit from cooler temperatures, the gravitational flow of water, and the semblance of seclusion. The surrounding, dry-laid stone wall forms a backdrop for an array of blooming plants, while the central, oval-shaped pool reflects the magnificence of the Conservatory rising in the background.

History: The Central Garden became a reality beginning in 2000, thanks to the generosity and vision of many. The North Terrace Garden was funded by the Vaughn-Jordan Foundation, while the Four Seasons Garden was made possible by Ann Lee Saunders Brown and Jane Quinn Saunders, sisters who provided gifts in memory of their mother, Janie Quinn Saunders. The Virginia Federation of Garden Clubs, Inc. funded the Healing Garden, and Alice and William Goodwin donated the Sunken Garden. Nearby, the Arbor Garden was given in memory of Josephine Cameron Rinckwitz by Viola Rinckwitz Wilbur and George W. Wilbur. Its complementing daffodil collection was given by friends and family of "Daffodil Lady" Suella Reynolds Robinson, who faithfully volunteered at the Garden for almost three decades. The Central Garden's numerous interconnecting paths with engraved bricks and pavers celebrate and commemorate countless individuals, families, and organizations that have generously chosen the Garden for their special tributes.

Education and Library Complex
CENTER FOR LEARNING

The Education and Library Complex (ELC) is the heart of learning at the Garden. Its architectural design is based on the proportions and scale of the Neo-Georgian Robins Visitors Center, while its exterior façade intentionally utilizes more glass as a segue to the classical, domed, glass Conservatory that resides nearby.

The building comprises thirty-two thousand square feet on two levels. The main level includes three wings: the **Joan Massey Conference Center** with its richly appointed auditorium and meeting rooms; the **Charles F. Gillette Education Center** with classroom and laboratory space; and the **Lora M. Robins Library** with more than seven thousand books, as well as collections of slides, videos, journals, and children's books. The Library's focus ranges from practical horticulture and botanical history to conservation and garden design, and includes 550 catalogs of current plant and seed sources. **Ginter Gallery II**, along the connecting hallway, centrally displays botanical art and seasonal exhibits. The first-floor's public spaces also enjoy scenic outdoor views and access to adjoining gardens.

Though not open to the public, the ELC's lower level houses the Garden's **archives**, rare books, and select art collections (*see* Special Collections). It also contains the **Herbarium Virginicum**, a cooperative initiative with Virginia Commonwealth University that preserves seventeen thousand dried plant specimens representing primarily native Virginia species, and four thousand specimens of mostly ornamental plants from the Garden's collection.

A central, covered portico entrance is graced by the **Evelyn G. Luck Garden**, whose elegant spaces are embraced by the building's symmetrical wings. This garden's formal boxwood border, groundcovers, ornate statuary, and proportions are inspired by the designs of Charles F. Gillette, Virginia's early twentieth-century master of landscape architecture.

History: The Education and Library Complex debuted in late 2002, providing the locus for the Garden's educational endeavors, as well as the community's business and social engagements. Primary donors were Lora M. Robins; the Massey Foundation in honor of Joan Massey; and the Mary Morton Parsons Foundation in honor of Charles F. Gillette. The Library's Reading Room was funded by Scott and Stringfellow, Inc.

Beautifying the building's exterior landscape, the Evelyn G. Luck Garden was given by Martha and C. B. Robertson III in memory of her mother, Evelyn G. Luck.

Leadership Donors for the construction of the Education and Library Complex included:

Alcoa	Media General
Bank of America	New Market
Brinks Company	Pauley Family Foundation
Circuit City Foundation	SunTrust Bank
Courtnay and Terrence Daniels	The Ukrop Foundation
	Wachovia Bank
Fort James Foundation	Windsor Foundation
Marietta M. and Samuel Tate Morgan Jr. Foundation	

• Annually, two thousand adults attend Lewis Ginter Botanical Garden's educational programs, while more than five hundred private rental events are hosted at the Garden by businesses, garden clubs, individuals, and community organizations.

• The Garden and the University of Richmond host a very successful certificate program in landscape design, while the Herbarium remains a valuable resource for Virginia Commonwealth University botany students and authors of *Flora of Virginia* (due for publication in 2012). The Garden also networks with J. Sargeant Reynolds Community College, Virginia Tech, and North Carolina State University, as well as other public gardens across the United States.

Conservatory
JEWEL OF THE GARDEN

Breathtaking. Dramatic and amazing. The Conservatory presides as the Garden's picturesque centerpiece, as well as one of the East Coast's few classically domed conservatories. Its jewel-box structure, which rises above an unbroken expanse of lawn, seems to float upon a green carpet for all to admire. A beautifully sculpted pineapple—the universal symbol for hospitality—crowns the sixty-three-foot-tall apex. The Conservatory's innumerable glass panes not only reflect light and beauty, they enclose ten thousand square feet of climate-controlled floral display areas.

The central **Palm House** greets guests with a vibrant fountain pool, ever-changing floral plantings, and a captivating collection of palm species from around the world.

Showcased in the **East Wing** is a spectacular orchid collection. From an assortment of nearly two thousand, each week those in full bloom are selected and displayed against the backdrop of a stone waterwall and pool, creating a haven rich in beauty and fragrance.

The **West Wing** houses the Garden Cottage with its charming thatched roof and surrounding garden-in-miniature. To the delight of visitors of all ages, children's literature often is interpreted in this area, linking the world of fantasy with the real world of living plants.

As a changeable display area, offerings in the **North Wing** vary throughout the year. During winter's GardenFest of Lights, model trains and a magnificent holiday tree are featured. Other times, the North Wing presents plants of economic importance and special exhibitions, such as "Butterflies LIVE!"

Heating: The Conservatory is entirely computer controlled to maintain ideal growing conditions in each area while optimizing energy efficiency. The Palm House and East Wing also have subsoil, hot-water heating tubes that ensure warm soil temperatures necessary for tropical species' survival. By warming the root zones, the plants tolerate much lower air temperatures, enabling the Garden to reduce fuel consumption and expense. Lower relative humidity further ensures fewer problems related to insects and disease.

Pest Management: Inevitably, insect populations infiltrate conservatory spaces and host themselves on the lush plants. The Garden responds with a system of integrated pest management that tolerates certain low-level or minimally-damaging populations of insect and disease; implements good growing practices; utilizes fans for air movement and reduced humidity levels; removes plants with greatest susceptibility to infection; uses beneficial insects as predators when possible; and relies on mechanical and pheromone lures to catch damaging insects.

History: Through the generous donations of Nancy and Bruce Gottwald; Libby and Floyd Gottwald; and the Gottwald Foundation, the Conservatory was completed in 2003 and dedicated to the memory of their mother, Anne Cobb Gottwald.

The pair of decorative urns that flank the Conservatory's entrance were given in 2004 by Henry Harrell and Anne Harrell Bristow in memory of their mother, Susan Haskell Harrell.

Construction of the Conservatory raised public awareness of Lewis Ginter Botanical Garden and transformed it into a four-season destination with regional significance. While its dome continues to enhance the Lakeside skyline, its iconic image symbolizes the Garden's enduring commitment to education, horticultural display, and year-round floral splendor.

Lewis Ginter Botanical Garden: 25 YEARS AND GROWING

Rose Garden
INDULGENCE FOR THE SENSES

Imagine the splendor and fragrance of almost two thousand rose bushes massed in a nine-thousand-square-foot hillside garden. This is the allure of the Rose Garden, which in 2008 was tripled in size, expanded in variety, and elevated to national significance.

Sensually enchanting, the Rose Garden entices visitors to pause, come close, and savor its offerings. Its arbors, stone arches, and pavilions are draped in more than eighty varieties of blooming roses that range from classic favorites to new hybrids, and unusual to rare specimens. The majority of cultivars originated from nurseries in France, Italy, Germany, and England, with an emphasis on genetically superior hybrids bred for disease resistance, rebloom, and fragrance. Environmental responsibility also guided selection, so as to reduce the need for fungicides. The garden's hillside location, which provides natural air movement, further minimizes the onset of fungal disease.

One unique aspect of the Rose Garden's design is its modulating color scheme. The central area is planted in whites and creams with pinks, purples, and reds graduating in intensity on one side, and yellows, apricots, and oranges graduating in intensity on the opposite. As the longest bloomed of flowering plants, this dynamic rose collection and its strategic plantings promise passers-by a long season of color and varied interest.

The Rose Garden also serves as an educational resource. Professional rosarians and amateurs alike can learn first-hand about the hybridizing, plant culture, and

rich history of the genus, which for centuries has been recognized as the symbol of love, life, and devotion.

The **terraced lawn** which tiers downhill from the Conservatory to the Rose Garden provides a spectacular setting for outdoor seating with panoramic views. The stone **belvedere** and its **terrace** were designed as a public centerpiece for the garden's performing arts programs and serve as a memorable venue for weddings and other private events.

History: Throughout her life, Louise B. Cochrane has expressed her admiration for roses through her paintings and personal gardens. In 2007, this "Lover of Roses" decided that the Richmond community would benefit from an expansion and reconfiguration of the Rose Garden and Belvedere that she originally funded in 2001. Her gift to the Garden transformed that dream to reality—now and for years to come thousands will delight in the roses due to Mrs. Cochrane's benevolence.

Henry M. Flagler Perennial Garden
ONE OF THE EAST COAST'S MOST DIVERSE PERENNIAL GARDENS

An expansive collection of perennials, bulbs, woody plants, and blooming shrubs reward Flagler Garden visitors with an ever-changing palette of seasonal beauty. Hostas, azaleas and rhododendrons, crape myrtles, and a plethora of ornamentals border a central grassy glen and adorn the landscape with a succession of multicolored blooms. Nearby, dwarf Japanese maples skirt the **Flagler Pavilion**, an elevated portico whose outstanding container gardens, vine-covered trellises, and stone archways exude a collective charm of their own. Mature tree canopies offer summer shade, while a splendid collection of ornamental grasses waves in the autumn breeze. Along the garden edge a pleasant stream meanders, nourishing plants and wildlife along its way. The Flagler Garden's three-acre haven also includes a cool, quiet woodland and the romantic, larger-than-life sculpture **Slow Dance.**

History: The Henry M. Flagler Perennial Garden was the gift of the Janet and Lawrence Lewis family through the Flagler Foundation. The garden was given in memory of their uncle Henry Morrison Flagler, who was a partner in Standard Oil and well known for his success in East Coast railway and real estate development—most famously, The Breakers Hotel in Palm Beach, Florida. The Lewises, lifelong residents of Richmond, sought opportunities to enhance their hometown and in 1990 decided to support the Flagler Garden as the first major project of the Garden's Master Plan. Endowment gifts that further supported the project were provided by Elizabeth (Leazie) and Jonathan Bryan III; Elizabeth (Betty) and Robert Pratt; and Kit and William Pannill.

Robert Hebb, who at that time was serving as the Garden's first executive director, was nationally renowned for his expertise in perennial plants. His passion inspired the use of perennials in the Flagler Garden design as a way to broaden the knowledge and use of herbaceous perennials in central Virginia. Through

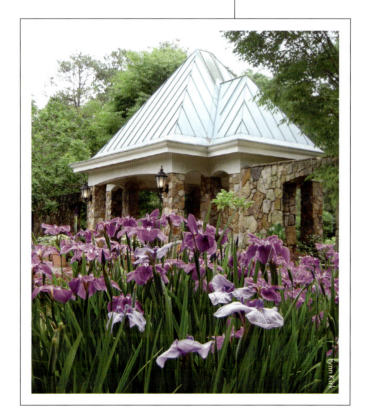

this focus, the Flagler Garden was both experimental and educational. Its dense understory of mixed herbaceous perennials is accented by flowering shrubs and trees.

Since its initial completion in 1993, the Flagler Garden has matured and naturally transformed from a sun garden to primarily a shade garden. Likewise, in recent years plant selections have transitioned toward perennials and shrubs that are shade-loving, yet new and interesting to Virginia gardens. Today, the Flagler Garden presents 1,278 unique types of plants.

Slow Dance: Charles B. Foster, grandson of Mr. and Mrs. Lewis, sculpted his artwork from North Carolina white granite. The sculpture was commissioned by Garland (Skip) S. Sydnor Jr. in honor of the Lewises for their generosity and in memory of his wife, Joyce Hunnicutt Sydnor. Mr. Sydnor served in various leadership capacities on the Garden's Board of Directors and as acting director from August 1991 to February 1992. Mrs. Sydnor was co-founder of the Bloemendaal Society, the garden's volunteer organization, and The Shop in the Garden (today's Garden Shop), for which she worked diligently until her untimely death.

Nancy Roberts Pope Memorial Narcissus Collection: Nancy Roberts Pope, whose favorite flower was the Poet's daffodils *(Narcissus poeticus)*, was a student in the Garden's landscape design program when she passed away from illness. Parents Jane and John Roberts established a fund in her memory, which has supported annual expansion of the daffodil collection for a decade. They also donated a charming curved bench and a wheelchair-accessible, paved walkway through the woodland garden where Mrs. Pope's engaging poem about her beloved flowers is cast in bronze for visitors to enjoy.

Clevenger Ornamental Grasses: The ornamental grasses gracing a sunlit spot along the central stream were given by Doris Clevenger in 2008. The collection was given in memory of her husband, Thomas Clevenger, a passionate gardener who was intrigued by ornamental grasses and personally collected them.

Dr. Irving Roberts Rhododendron Collection: A variety of flowering rhododendrons and allied plants were planted in memory of Dr. Irving Roberts, an early member of the Garden's Board of Directors. The donor was his wife, Doris Roberts, a friend of the Garden and leader of the Ikebana of Richmond organization.

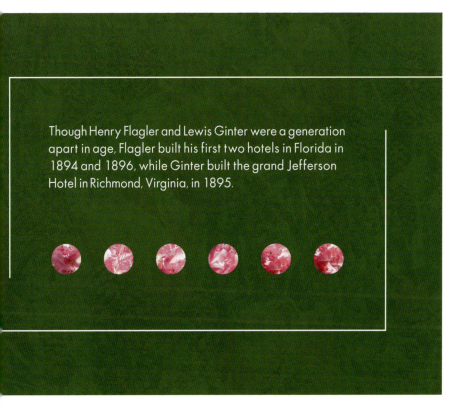

Though Henry Flagler and Lewis Ginter were a generation apart in age, Flagler built his first two hotels in Florida in 1894 and 1896, while Ginter built the grand Jefferson Hotel in Richmond, Virginia, in 1895.

Rob's Garden: At the Flagler Garden's northern edge, an intimate garden and gazebo were donated by the family of Christopher Robins (Rob) Haskell in honor of his life. Mr. Haskell, who tragically passed away in his twenties, was the grandson of the garden's generous benefactors Lora M. and E. Claiborne Robins Sr.

For enhancement of the visitor experience, **Flagler Pavilion lighting** was presented by Ethel Mahone and Wirt Atkinson Christian Sr., and **garden benches** were provided by Nathalie and Philip Klaus Sr.

Asian Valley
PEACE WITH NATURE

Stroll the Asian Valley to experience the joy of tranquility, the beauty of simplicity, and harmony with nature. Notice shallow streams that soften rock-strewn landscapes while gently cascading into placid, reflective pools. Journey across inviting stepping stones, wooden bridges, and winding walkways to see dramatic tree forms, including handsome Japanese maples and richly textured conifers. Marvel at striking Japanese irises and camellias, a fine collection of peonies, and other enchanting East Asian plants. Pause to watch fauna that is attracted to the rich, inviting environment. Admire stone sculptures and classical lanterns that reflect oriental art and culture.

And, visit the **Lora and Claiborne Robins Tea House** that presides over the Garden as a delightful restaurant with panoramic views of nature's year-round splendor.

History: In 1993, when the Bloemendaal House was the Garden's only building and the Flagler Garden was near completion, donors voiced a desire for a dining facility to support increased visitation. A planned ten-by-ten-foot replica of a Japanese tea house and raked gravel Zen garden became the inspiration for the restaurant. Initial designs called for the eatery to overlook the central lake (where the CWDKids Tree House now stands), but building codes and limited infrastructure precluded use of that location, so everything changed—and for the better. The project moved to its current site at the Garden's eastern boundary; the plan expanded to a full-service, seventy-five-seat restaurant; and the design reflected Japanese architectural elements and scale. Ever the visionaries, Lora M. and E. Claiborne Robins Sr. funded the project.

Two years later, following the death of Mr. Robins, additional gifts were provided by his wife for design of the Asian Valley as a complement to the Tea House. The Garden's flora—native to Japan, China, and Korea—was selected for aesthetics and uniqueness, as well as compatibility with the central Virginia climate. Continued generosity from Ikebana of Richmond has supported expansion of the Japanese iris collection.

Lewis Ginter Botanical Garden: 25 YEARS AND GROWING

Lewis Ginter Botanical Garden: 25 YEARS AND GROWING

Martha and Reed West Island Garden
DIVERSE AND RICHLY PLANTED WETLAND

Three small islands in the east lake, linked by a series of wooden bridges and boardwalks, bid exploration of the West Island Garden. With a wet, bog-like environment, the area provides a diverse ecosystem for both plant life and wildlife. Most of this garden's plant species are either native to the eastern United States or hybrids derived from native plants. Especially intriguing is the West Island's impressive collection of the *Sarracenia* or pitcher plant, the insectivorous (insect eating) genus that derives nitrogen from digested insects captured in its "throat." The West Island Garden also teems with wildlife that never hesitates to make an appearance. Fish, toads, and turtles bask in the sun's rays, chipmunks scamper, and a near-tame Great Blue Heron proudly calls the garden home.

History: Martha West served as a longtime member of the Garden's Board of Directors. When Lora M. and E. Claiborne Robins Sr. gave their gift to construct the Tea House, Mrs. West wished to ensure there were beautiful views from the Tea House windows and deck. She and her husband, Reed, chose to fund this new wetland garden in 1993. Their foresight transformed the area into a much-loved destination.

In addition to creating a beautiful vista and rich habitat for native flora and local fauna, the West Island Garden reflects Mr. West's personal history. A native of South Carolina's tidal marshlands, Mr. West was intrigued to re-create a landscape close to his heart. He was particularly pleased with the addition of the native *Taxodium distichum* or bald cypress, a tree that grew on lands owned by his family during his youth.

Lewis Ginter Botanical Garden: 25 YEARS AND GROWING

Lewis Ginter Botanical Garden: 25 YEARS AND GROWING

Bloemendaal House
AMID A VALLEY OF FLOWERS

"Bloemendaal," Dutch for "valley of flowers," is a fitting name for the Garden's historic landmark. It is named after a village in western Holland, the ancestral home of the Ginter family. Its setting abounds with mature trees, flowering shrubs, and perennials. Though the three-story Dutch Colonial generally is not open for public visitation, the spacious first-floor rooms are available for rental.

The house's four-thousand-square-foot interior is embellished with period antiques and furnishings reminiscent of the Arts and Crafts era. The main parlor, a sizeable room off the front veranda, features well-appointed seating and a central, red-brick fireplace accentuated by the original handcrafted brass "Bloemendaal" medallion with elegant cast-iron detailing. Iron chandeliers and sconces emanate history through lighting fashioned decades ago by Richmond's own Tredegar Iron Works. A luxurious dining room with a cherry dining table and antique sideboard is illuminated by a crystal chandelier salvaged from a grand, historic home of old Richmond. Nearby, cozy side parlors extend comfortable, fireside seating for private meetings and events. Hallway galleries and lighted display cases showcase art and exquisite porcelain collections (*see* Special Collections). Throughout the Bloemendaal House, rich wood paneling, high ceilings, an original stained-glass skylight, and other European-influenced details contribute to the gracious ambiance. Oversized windows bring the outdoors in, imparting views of Lakeside Lake, the Wildside Walk, and the resplendent Grace Arents Garden.

Lewis Ginter Botanical Garden: 25 YEARS AND GROWING

History: In 1884, prosperous businessman Lewis Ginter built the original one-story structure as a part of the multiplex community destination named Lakeside Park, which included a zoo, boating lake, and casino. He constructed a narrow-gauge railroad from the intersection of Hermitage and Laburnum Avenues, where it connected to the Richmond streetcar system so gents and belles could easily travel to the then rural setting. Called Lakeside Wheel Club, the building initially served as a gathering place for bicyclists, the trendy pastime of the 1890s. After Ginter's death, his niece Grace Arents bought the structure, added the second story, and used it as a convalescent home for urban children who were ill. In 1917, it once again was refurbished as Grace Arents' personal home, where she lived until her death in 1926 (*see* The Garden's History).

Grace Arents Garden
VICTORIAN GARDEN

Romantically elegant, the Grace Arents Garden epitomizes a typical early twentieth-century, late-Victorian garden. Traditional boxwood borders, fastidiously sculpted topiaries, period-appropriate plants, and a plethora of climbing roses upon white, latticed arches—all evoke old-fashioned charm. Based on historic photographs, today's Grace Arents Garden features gazebo and arbor seating, as well as cobbled brick walks that access the formal garden spaces. The Garden's centerpiece, a decorative sundial, is a 1914 original feature from Miss Grace's own garden (*see* The Garden's History). As the Grace Arents Garden reflects a time in history, it beautifies the Bloemendaal House and serves as an enchanting venue for weddings and special events.

History: In 1990, the Garden Club of Virginia completed revitalization of the Grace Arents Garden as their annual historic restoration project in the Commonwealth. Their support created the first extant garden, following the 1984 chartering of Lewis Ginter Botanical Garden.

Lewis Ginter Botanical Garden: 25 YEARS AND GROWING

Miss Grace's 1914 sundial

Friendship Garden
THRESHOLD TO THE BLOEMENDAAL HOUSE

At the historic Bloemendaal House main entrance, a garden-in-miniature extends greetings—both then and now.

History: A century ago, horse-drawn carriages traveled the same route as the paved drive that today leads from Lakeside Avenue to the Bloemendaal House. The portal's original steps, newel posts, inlaid leaf-patterned walks, and cast-iron Victorian lampposts still remain today. The Garden itself was created in the early 1980s by the Richmond Horticultural Association in memory of Madeline W. Livesay, garden writer for the Richmond newspapers, 1970 "Virginia Press Woman of the Year," and friend of the Garden.

Wildside Walk
FOOTPATH ALONG LAKE'S EDGE

Tucked behind the Bloemendaal House, the Wildside Walk's naturalistic hillside and meandering path overlook Lakeside Lake, formerly a millpond and then a boating lake in Ginter's time. Today, North American wildflowers, azaleas, and rhododendrons decorate the wooded nature trail, while a cool microclimate supports mosses, lichens, unusual ferns, and an abundance of wildlife. Bird watchers and observant trekkers also discover remnants of a nineteenth-century woodland garden, including a frog-ornamented stone fountain—a forerunner to the frog fountain in today's Four Seasons Garden.

History: Grace Arents frequented this hillside in the early 1900s, so a journey along its paths is indeed a walk in her historic footsteps (*see* The Garden's History). However, through the years the Garden expanded the varieties of woodland species through additional plantings and "plant rescue" collaborations with developers of Wintergreen Resort in Virginia's Blue Ridge Mountains.

Miss Grace's frog fountain

Bloemendaal's original hillside

Lace House

WOODLAND RESTING PLACE

Set off slightly east is the Lace House Garden and gazebo. Its tranquil setting offers seclusion, shade from a mature tree canopy, and natural beauty from surrounding azalea and woodland gardens.

History: Originally called Summerhouse, the intricate white pergola was hand-carved in 1800 for Samuel Myers' Governor Street garden. It was relocated to Lewis Ginter Botanical Garden in 1994, through a gift from the Historic Richmond Association, and then restored through the support of the Jeffress Foundation. The surrounding azaleas, known as the **Christian Family Azalea Collection**, were funded by Beverly Inge and Wirt Christian in 1995 in memory of her mother, Mary Stine Seal. Along the woodland border is the **Van Arnam Memorial Garden,** given in 1996 by Joan Foster Van Arnam and William L. Van Arnam in memory of Carlyn Manifold Foster and Dr. John VanValzah Foster. Dr. Foster was an avid Pennsylvania gardener who enjoyed hybridizing Rhododendrons and other Ericaceous species.

The adjoining lawn, between the forest edge and the Bloemendaal House drive, is the setting for a **unique collection of trees** that originated from around the world. The gingko, Norway spruce, hemlock, and Japanese plum yew were planted by Grace Arents, who was inspired by her international travels. Unusual specimens at that time, this collection became one of Virginia's earliest arboretums (*see* The Garden's History).

Children's Garden
WHERE YOUNGSTERS EXPLORE THE WONDERS OF NATURE

A place where kids can be kids. An outdoor "living classroom" where learning is natural. A safe haven for exploration and unstructured play. A three-acre habitat where an appreciation for gardening develops and stewardship rules. A gathering place that fosters interactive adventures and intergenerational fun. A landscape of diversity which celebrates the global richness of cultures, plants, ecosystems, habitats, and adaptation. All this and more describe the Children's Garden—one of the region's most-popular, most-visited family destinations.

The Children's Garden is designed so youngsters can experience the great outdoors—by observing wildlife; digging in the dirt; climbing a one-hundred-year-old mulberry tree; or simply doing nothing at all. The area's permanent features include the **International Village**, which brings the world home through globally inspired architectures, cultures, and indigenous plants. The **Adventure Pathway** winds among prairie, butterfly meadow, and evergreen environs, while the universally accessible **Leafy Overlook** and **CWDKids Tree House** reveal the world from a bird's-eye view. **WaterPlay** refreshes with cooling fountains and carefree sprays. **Weird and Contrasting Plants** illustrates nature's amazing diversities and adaptations to environment, while the **Greenhouse** demonstrates propagation and planting techniques. The Jane Quinn Saunders **Farm Garden** invites children to plant and nurture wholesome fruits and vegetables, with several hundred pounds annually donated to the feeding of central Virginia's hungry children. During summer months, the **Activity Center** encourages exploration of animals, weather, and natural materials in the property's original Carriage House, as the **Central Plaza** hosts special programs and

Lewis Ginter Botanical Garden: 25 YEARS AND GROWING

performances. The Garden Keeper's Cottage is staged for playtime any time, and sometimes the Garden Keeper herself makes a visit. The **Garden Cart, Investigation Station**, and **Kids Quest**—plus student workshops, camps, and family events—round out the educational offerings and contribute to the year-round fun.

History: The historical roots of the Children's Garden extend back almost one hundred years to the days of Grace Arents, the niece and heir of Lewis Ginter. When Arents converted the Wheel Club to a children's convalescent home, she also grew fresh produce for its residents at the current site of the Children's Garden. Known as a progressive gardener, Arents received visitors who wanted to see the latest varieties and

For more than two decades, the growth and expansion of Lewis Ginter Botanical Garden relied on the generosity of key philanthropists. The Children's Garden was the first fundraising campaign in the Garden's history whose success resulted from broad-based community support. Its stakeholders include these Leadership Donors:

Mr. Beverley W. Armstrong
Ms. Susan H. Armstrong
Mr. and Mrs. Roger L. Boeve
Ann Lee Saunders Brown
The Cabell Foundation
Children's Wear Digest
The Community Foundation
CSX Corporation
Professor and Mrs. Robert C. Dolan
Mrs. Joan M. Ferrill
Mr. and Mrs. Robert V. Hatcher Jr.
Henrico County
Mrs. Anne M. Jones
Klaus Family
Mr. and Mrs. Philip W. Klaus Sr.
Mr. and Mrs. Bertrand Latil
The Lipman Foundation
Marietta M. and Samuel Tate Morgan Jr. Foundation
Massey Foundation
Mrs. Alfred McCormack Jr.
The Memorial Foundation for Children, 200th Anniversary Commemorative Gift
Mr. and Mrs. Lewis N. Miller Jr.
NELCO Family Foundation
Mr. and Mrs. Richard A. Nelson
Mr. and Mrs. Theodore W. Price
Miss Noelwa C. Ratcliffe
Richard and Caroline T. Gwathmey Memorial Trust
Richard S. Reynolds Foundation
Robins Foundation
Jane Quinn Saunders
Mr. and Mrs. John W. Snow
Mr. and Mrs. Wallace Stettinius
Thomas F. Jeffress Memorial, Inc.
Mr. and Mrs. Matthew G. Thompson
Thompson, Siegel and Walmsley, Inc.
Tilghman Family Foundation
Wachovia Foundation
Wachovia Securities
Mrs. Thomas F. Wheeldon
Mrs. James L. Wiley
The William H.-John G.-Emma Scott Foundation
Windsor Foundation, Inc.

techniques. The old red mulberry tree would have been grown for its abundant fruit and most likely survives from this period. The Carriage House, which now serves as the center for children's education, was used for the storage and care of Arents' carriages. Its tower housed a giant water tank, used for domestic needs, irrigation, and a rare private fire-hydrant system. The water tank was sacrificed in World War II to provide metal for the war effort.

The first Children's Garden, a more modest learning environment, was developed at this location in 1995 through funding by the Memorial Foundation for Children. Its popularity, visitation, and community research soon validated the need for expansion. In 1997, the Garden launched its first major capital campaign, "A Growing Vision," which enjoyed vigorous support from the Richmond community. The 2005 unveiling of the Children's Garden honored Arents' love of nature and children. It also forever changed the Garden landscape, as well as its member demographics and impact on future generations. Shortly thereafter, Jane Quinn Saunders bequeathed a generous endowment for the ongoing care of this area. Her legacy positively impacts thousands of youngsters and families who visit each year.

Sydnor Lake
MIRRORING NATURE'S BEAUTY

Sydnor Lake is a home to wildlife; a reservoir for the garden's irrigation system; and a visual transition from land to water gardens. Beautifully responding to the variable seasons and shifting sunlight, the lake also provides a fascinating backdrop for artists and photographers.

History: Understanding that water is critical to the Garden's continued success and recognizing a need to manage its surface water, the lake was the first step in fulfillment of the Garden's 1987 Master Plan. Constructed in 1989, the lake quickly defined the new heart of the Garden as it teemed with wildlife and natural beauty. Its construction was carefully overseen by Garland (Skip) S. Sydnor Jr., a member of the Garden's board, a hydrology engineer, and business owner whose family had spent lifetimes in the construction of lakes, wells, and water systems.

Sydnor was so dedicated to Lewis Ginter Botanical Garden that in 1991, upon the departure of the Garden's first director, Robert Hebb, Sydnor accepted the role of acting director and chair of the search committee for more than six months. He also inherited management of the just-initiated construction of the Flagler Garden. Over the years, Sydnor served in many capacities on the Board of Directors, including president and chair of the planning committee. He guided the development of the Garden's irrigation system and the addition of a second lake to source today's Garden-wide irrigation, plus contributed significantly to the 2006 hydrological Master Plan. During Sydnor's many years of committed service, he provided the Garden with numerous generous gifts in various forms. In 2006, Sydnor Lake was dedicated in honor of Garland (Skip) S. Sydnor Jr. in recognition of his long-term service and abundant generosity.

Lewis Ginter Botanical Garden: 25 YEARS AND GROWING

Lucy Payne Minor Memorial Garden
DELIGHTFUL DAFFODILS AND DAYLILIES

"... and dances with the daffodils," an excerpt from William Wordsworth's 1804 poem "Daffodils," is cast on a bronze plaque in the Minor Memorial Garden. This poignant phrase expresses the heartfelt joy that arises whenever one discovers "a crowd, A host of golden daffodils." Representing wild indigenous forms to modern hybrids, the Minor Memorial Garden's collections of daffodils and daylilies provide more than just beauty. They also encourage an intriguing exploration of the hand of man in cultivating and breeding plants over the centuries. An inviting gazebo, tucked among the perennials, ornamental shrubs, and trees, also lends character to this lovely lakeside retreat.

History: Philip M. Minor funded the garden in memory of his wife, Lucy Payne Minor. During her lifetime, Mrs. Minor was revered as a talented flower arranger and Garden Club of America judge.

Margaret Johanna Streb Conifer Garden
CONIFERS WITH YEAR-ROUND INTEREST

Encounter an attractive blend of diverse and fascinating dwarf conifers, complemented by ornamental grasses and spring-blooming minor bulbs, in the Streb Conifer Garden. Through myriad forms, sizes, and hues these conifers demonstrate practical uses for providing structure, color, and texture in the garden—as well as year-round interest. A gazebo, architecturally inspired by the Bloemendaal House, imparts an open invitation to stop and peruse the views.

History: In 1996, Jacquie and Ben White provided the funding for this conifer garden and gazebo in honor of Mrs. White's mother, Margaret Johanna Streb. The Whites were inspired by the Gotelli Collection of dwarf conifers at the U.S. National Arboretum in Washington, D.C.

Hal Tyler

Vienna Cobb Anderson Wildflower Meadow
HILLSIDE GRACED BY WILDFLOWERS

Evolving season by season, the Wildflower Meadow overlooks Sydnor Lake's southern edge. The meadow's rich herbaceous environment supports plantings of colorful flowering annuals and perennials that peak late spring through summer. A unique demonstration of a meadow habitat, this hillside is home to native and exotic plant species, as well as butterflies, birds, bees, and other pollinating insects and small vertebrates.

History: Pauline (Polly) and Robert Anderson III funded this naturalistic, lakeside planting in memory of Mr. Anderson's mother.

ANNE HOLT MASSEY GREENHOUSES
NURTURING PLANTS AND RESEARCH

The ten-thousand-square-foot Massey Greenhouses, which are of Dutch design and fully automated, serve vital functions as centers for propagation and research; areas for the care of permanent non-hardy collections; and growing houses for the Garden volunteers' semiannual plant sales.

History: Anne Holt Massey, longtime Board member and noted gardener, was the namesake and donor of this range of greenhouses. Located just northwest of the Conservatory, these working greenhouses are closed to visitors.

LOCBURY HOUSE

Similar in age to the Bloemendaal House, the historic Locbury House is situated on Locbury Lane near the Garden's northwestern boundary. Through the decades, this residence was adapted to the Garden's ever-changing needs—ranging from housing for the first director, visiting researchers and interns, to current offices for the Horticulture Department. Though not open to the public, the Dutch Colonial structure serves as another reminder of the Garden's rich history.

PERIMETER LANDSCAPE AND ENTRANCE

A "living billboard" of flowering plants welcomes visitors as they approach the Garden's perimeter, fronting the intersection of Lakeside Avenue and Hilliard Road. Flowering apricots peek through the chill in late February; winter jasmine, forsythia, and daffodils burst forth in spring; crape myrtles welcome summer with bloom-filled branches; vibrantly colored leaves announce autumn; and evergreen, deciduous holly, and red twig dogwoods impart visual sustenance during winter.

History: Henrico County funded this four-season perimeter to beautify the Lakeside District and to support the endeavors of Lewis Ginter Botanical Garden.

Special Collections

BOTANICAL ILLUSTRATIONS

Descubes Botanical Art: Rich in beauty and significance is the Garden's prized collection of twenty-five hundred original botanical illustrations by Alexandre Descubes. Most of the artworks, dated between 1875 and 1919, represent plants that Descubes found growing on the Indian subcontinent, with a few reflecting flora of Pakistan, Sikkim, Bhutan, Nepal, the Himalayas, and the Malayan Peninsula. Each illustration was drawn in pencil, painted in watercolor, and then annotated with extensive botanical information, a full botanical description, and a listing of countries or habitats in which the plant was distributed. Especially useful to historians and anthropologists is that each plant's name is listed in its local vernacular. Many of the detailed renderings also include inked impressions of leaves for the visual recording of size and veining.

Currently, fifty Descubes originals are displayed in the Garden Café and Visitors Center, while the remaining collection is viewable by appointment with the Garden librarian. Both yesteryear and today, the Descubes collection proves remarkable as a botanical reference and a treasured work of art.

History: Alexandre Descubes was born in the early 1850s on the island of Mauritius, located in the Indian Ocean. In 1874, he was appointed draughtsman in that country's Public Works Department, where he served as a land surveyor and cartographer. Years later, Descubes was employed as superintendent of map records with the Forest Survey of India. The Garden's extensive Descubes collection was generously donated by Lora M. Robins, who recognized its historical, botanical, and artistic value.

Mary Vaux Walcott Botanical Prints: Also available for viewing by appointment are watercolor prints of North American wildflowers by American naturalist and artist Mary Vaux Walcott (1860–1940). The Garden's 225-print collection originates from a set of 400 published by the Smithsonian Institution. The Walcott prints were a gift from Edward W. Rucker.

Mark Catesby Illustrations: Displayed in the Bloemendaal House are four original illustrations by Mark Catesby, a celebrated eighteenth-century English naturalist who traveled and recorded the native flora and fauna of the Virginia colony. Garland S. Sydnor Jr. provided these gifts.

Orchid Watercolors: Intermingled among the Catesby illustrations are more than a dozen orchid watercolors, a donation from former Board member Tazwell (Taz) M. Carrington III.

HISTORICAL PAINTINGS

The family heirloom that hangs in the Bloemendaal House dining room is an **oil painting of Jane Ginter Arents**, the mother of Grace Arents and sister of Lewis Ginter.

Gracing the Bloemendaal's main hallway is another artistic treasure: a **watercolor print of Sydney Harbour**, presented to Lewis Ginter by staff and officials when he visited Australia during that county's 1888 centennial celebration.

BOOKS

R. Eldridge Longest bequeathed 286 volumes on herbs and medicinal plants to the Lora M. Robins Library, as well as an endowment to ensure that the library's technology and distribution of knowledge remains relevant and current.

BOTANICAL PORCELAINS

Patrick O'Hara Botanical Sculptures: The conservation of plants in their own natural habitats is the inspiration for Ireland's celebrated sculptor Patrick O'Hara. Five of O'Hara's life-size, original porcelain masterpieces of the native flora of Virginia, representing diverse natural regions of the state, were donated in the late 1980s by Lora M. Robins.

Boehm Porcelains: More than sixty Boehm Porcelains, given to the Garden by Martha West and Lora M. Robins, are showcased in the Bloemendaal House and the Visitors Center. Each sculpture's exquisite detail and quality craftsmanship result from skilled artisans using porcelain processes that originated in ancient China.

"Blue Ridge Fire," 1989 by Patrick O'Hara

THE GARDEN'S HISTORY

Stroll back in time to late nineteenth-century Richmond, Virginia—the age of farms and factories, Civil War and Reconstruction, bustling city centers and streetcar suburbs. This was the era of Major Lewis Ginter—a brilliant businessman, refined gentleman, and generous philanthropist whose influence continues today.

Ginter's was a life of contrasts—a series of accomplishments and failures, poverty and wealth. His interests were diverse, his character complex. Yet at the time of his death in 1897, *The Evening Leader* front-page news story extolled Ginter as Richmond's "foremost citizen in wealth and public spirit." Likewise, business and social leaders praised Ginter's contributions to the city's economic growth, residential development, and cultural enrichment.

The story of Lewis Ginter, along with his niece Grace Arents, is significant because it is much more than the chronicle of one man or one family. It is the rich history of Richmond—and the foundation for appreciating one of today's most-visited regional attractions: Lewis Ginter Botanical Garden.

Lewis Ginter
THE BOTANICAL GARDEN'S NAMESAKE

His Youth: Lewis Ginter, born in 1824 in New York City, was the fifth and youngest child of John Ginter and Eliza Somerindyke. The family's original surname "Guenther" was Americanized as "Ginter" during his grandfather's day, but Lewis always remembered his Dutch-immigrant roots.

Orphaned at age eleven and reared by his older sister Jane, Ginter's formal education ended when he was just twelve years old. Though nearly penniless and barely educated, Ginter confidently struck out on his own at age seventeen, moving south to the burgeoning city of Richmond, Virginia. The young entrepreneur's first business endeavor was a variety store,

then known as a "Yankee notion house," located on Main Street. His signature use of attractive wrapping papers and creative packaging became as popular as the toys, domestic articles, and toiletries that he sold. The savvy retailer soon added imported linens and woolens to his line of merchandise, thereby expanding marketshare. Sales soared, and Ginter amassed a fortune of $200,000 by the start of the Civil War.

Civil War and Reconstruction: When war erupted, thirty-seven-year-old Ginter sold his retail business and invested in sugar, cotton, and tobacco. Though a Northerner by birth, he actively supported the Southern cause by buying bonds and joining the army of the Confederate States. Appointed commissary, he earned the nickname "The Fighting Commissary." Later, declining a promotion to brigadier, Ginter accepted the rank of major under General A. P. Hill, and for the remainder of his life he was addressed as Major Ginter.

During the Confederate evacuation of 1865, much of Richmond was burned, as were Ginter's warehouses of sugar and tobacco. Fortunately his cotton escaped destruction, providing him a small capital to finance his return to New York City. There he entered the world of banking and brokerage and methodically built his second fortune—only to lose $300,000 in 1873 due to a partner's incompetence and the "Black Friday" stock market crash. Ginter demonstrated his integrity when he later not only repaid all creditors, but did so with compounded interest.

Tobacco King: Fifty years old and financially ruined, Ginter again relocated to Richmond where he hoped to regain the prosperity and contentment enjoyed in former years. With an aptitude for sales, Ginter accepted tobacco consignments on behalf of Southern growers and not surprisingly, his third fortune was made in short time. Accepting a partnership offer from John F. Allen, Ginter then broadened his horizons by traveling the world to promote "Richmond Gems." These cigarettes were made with Virginia tobacco and hand rolled by young ladies, making theirs the first company in the south to employ women in cigarette manufacturing. Ginter enhanced the

cigarettes' appeal by developing another first: collectible "trading cards" for enclosure in each cigarette package. Some card series featured renderings of lovely women, while others highlighted sports memorabilia. Ginter's marketing idea was ingenious, the cigarettes' popularity strong, and resulting sales sensational. To meet rising demand, Allen and Ginter offered a $75,000 prize to anyone inventing an automated cigarette-making machine. Over the next nine years, mechanization and marketing grew their tobacco enterprise into one of the nation's largest. In 1890, Allen and Ginter merged with four other manufacturers: W. Duke, Sons and Company; William S. Kimball and Company; Kinney Tobacco; and Goodwin and Company to form the American Tobacco Company, a forerunner of today's Philip Morris USA.

Richmond Legacies: Several other leading corporations and historic landmarks trace their lineage back to Major Ginter. During the last decade of his life, known as the Gilded Age, this self-made millionaire purchased the *Richmond Daily Times* newspaper (which he later gave to his attorney and friend Joseph Bryan as the beginnings of the *Richmond Times-Dispatch* and Media General); personally financed and supervised construction of the majestic Jefferson Hotel; supported numerous churches and charities; and gifted land for Joseph Bryan Park and Union Theological Seminary when the latter moved from Hampden-Sydney College. In addition, he donated land and was instrumental in the construction of the monument to General A. P. Hill at Hermitage Road and Laburnum Avenue, which remains Richmond's only monument where a Civil War general is buried.

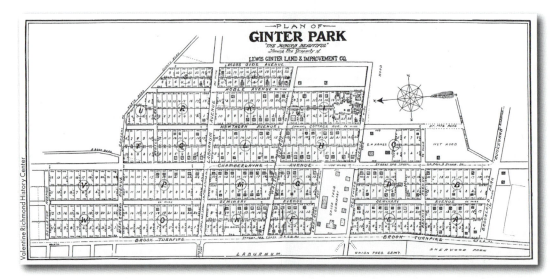

Another of Ginter's endeavors was fueled by acquisition of vast acreage in Richmond's Northside and his 1888 visit to Australia. Having admired artistically landscaped, master-planned communities in Adelaide, Sydney, and Melbourne, in a similar fashion the real estate mogul developed three Richmond neighborhoods: Bellevue Park, Sherwood Park, and Ginter Park. Each suburb was planted with miles of shrubs and trees, ensuring picturesque settings along with conveniences of urban life. Ginter Park, in particular, earned distinction as "Queen of the Suburbs." Its landscape plan was the work of Frederick Law Olmsted, the renowned founder of American landscape architecture who also designed the grounds of Asheville's Biltmore Estate and New York City's Central Park.

Lewis Ginter developed Richmond's Ginter Park streetcar community; invested in America's first citywide electric streetcar system; and commissioned construction of the renowned Jefferson Hotel, c. 1895.

Even Richmond transportation benefited from Ginter's journeys and innovations. Inspired by India's narrow-gauge railroads that transported sugarcane, Ginter constructed a similar railway system in Richmond's Northside in 1892. His commissioning of a narrow-gauge railway, which replaced mules for hauling stone from the Bryan Park quarry to his Ginter Park suburb, spurred development of the Richmond Locomotive Works. Meanwhile, Ginter's locomotive "Barbara" transported city dwellers to his lakeside retreat. In 1897, Ginter and the Richmond Railway and Electric Company (its electricity generation plant the precursor of Dominion Virginia Power) distinguished Richmond as the nation's first city with an electric streetcar system.

Richmond's social scene was enhanced following Ginter's purchase of ten acres overlooking Ufton Brook. After damming the waterway to form Lakeside Lake, Ginter constructed the Lakeside Wheel Club in 1894 as a gathering place for sports cyclists and socially minded belles. Cyclists peddled to the recreational resort along the Missing Link Trail, which paralleled the Boulevard and Hermitage Road, while spectators rode the Lakeside trolley. During the Gay Nineties, Richmonders congregated at the one-story Victorian club house to enjoy freshly made ice cream and charming lakeside views (see The Garden Today, Bloemendaal House). Another fashionable entertainment destination emerged with Ginter's development of Lakeside Park, now the site of Jefferson-Lakeside Country Club. Featuring a zoo and the city's first public nine-hole golf course, the attraction grew in regional popularity. The newspaper recorded the Park's grand opening: "Within the enclosure are two large sheets of water, the clubhouse of the Lakeside bicycle club, a casino, café, bowling alley, billiard rooms, deer house, park office, and apartments for officers. The lake . . . specially stocked with fish . . . [is] supplied with an abundance of rowboats and a speedy two-horse-power naphtha launch" (*Richmond Dispatch*, March 15, 1896).

The Next Generation: Major Ginter always remembered the nurturing his older sister Jane provided when they were orphaned in his youth. Almost four decades later when Jane's husband died, Ginter invited the widow and her four children to make their home with him in Richmond. Quite naturally, the children grew in admiration and affection for Uncle Lewis, and the life of one—young Grace Arents—was forever changed.

Lakeside Wheel Club, c. 1894.

When Major Ginter died in 1897, he was buried at Richmond's Hollywood Cemetery. A magnificent mausoleum, embellished with exquisite Tiffany stained-glass windows, still stands in tribute to Ginter's enthusiastic vision, enduring contributions, and endless generosity. At his death, a Northern newspaper proclaimed Ginter "the richest man south of the Potomac," and almost every charitable institution in the city was remembered in his will. The confirmed bachelor magnanimously bequeathed his fortune, estimated at seven to ten million dollars, to the city he loved and to his beloved niece Grace.

Ginter Park, "Queen of the Suburbs," at the crossroads of Seminary and Laburnum Avenues (1900).

Grace Evelyn Arents
A FAMILY'S LEGACY CONTINUES

Perhaps no one influenced Grace Arents as much as her Uncle Lewis Ginter, who was her elder by only twenty-four years. With apparent devotion, Ginter showed Arents the world, fostered her curiosity in horticulture, and nurtured her dedication to philanthropy. Ginter also may have encouraged the independent young maiden to confidently follow her interests and dreams—a novel mind-set for women of that era. Like Ginter's legacy, Arents' influence lives on today.

Miss Grace: Born in New York in 1848, Arents moved to Richmond sometime in her mid-twenties following her father's death. Her personal life remains an enigma, for though she contributed much to the city of Richmond throughout her lifetime, she shared little about herself in the process. Historical narratives describe Arents as "small of stature, with thick glasses." Little else is known about her physical characteristics, for she modestly avoided being photographed most of her life. However, her personality and character were demonstrated through her many business dealings, volunteer endeavors, and charitable gifts. When she died of a heart attack in 1926, the Richmond community deeply respected the woman they called "Miss Grace." Arents was interred at Hollywood Cemetery in a modest grave near her beloved uncle's resplendent mausoleum.

Benevolence and Bloemendaal Farm: The foundation for Arents' charitable generosity was her belief that her inheritance was a custodial duty. Her munificence in the Oregon Hill District, where the urban working class lived, included personal financing and construction of St. Andrew's Episcopal Church (Virginia's first Episcopal church with free pews), the tuition-free St. Andrew's School, affordable housing, public bathhouses, and Richmond's first free library.

Trained as a nurse, in 1913, Arents turned her attention to sick children who struggled with illnesses related to the city's pollution and overcrowded conditions. Convinced that a

fresh country environment would support recuperation, Arents purchased approximately ten acres and the abandoned Lakeside Wheel House in the city's Northside. She remodeled her uncle's former club house in a Dutch colonial style and removed the roof to add a second story for bedrooms, classroom, playroom, and library. Gardens were developed for beauty and food production, and the convalescent complex was appropriately named "Bloemendaal"—Dutch for "valley of flowers"—in tribute to her family's ancestry.

Another health-related contribution was Arents' involvement in founding the Instructive Visiting Nurse Association. This healthcare initiative eventually ended the need for a children's convalescent center, so the Bloemendaal House became available in 1917 as the primary residence for Arents and Mary Garland Smith, who was her companion and a St. Andrews School teacher.

Global Travel, Global Horticulture: Miss Grace discovered the joy of travel in her early forties. Her 1888 travel diary, "Grace Notes," recorded that on "Thursday June 14th Uncle Lewis and I left Richmond on the 11 AM train—starting on what may be a trip around the world." Their journey took them to Honolulu where they "were full of admiration of the wonderful tropical gamut we saw—cocoa date & royal palms—banana breadfruit, mangoe among the fruit trees, & numbers of flowering trees . . . [which were] simply gorgeous." Their steamer, which Arents called a "floating hotel," transported them on to Australia where they were "charmed by the botanical garden . . . with green house after green house filled with palm, ferns, [and] plants with colored leaves," as well as suburbs "laid off with beautifully broad streets bordered with trees" of strange varieties.

Miss Grace extensively traveled.

Fascinated by the flora and landscapes seen abroad, Arents collected tree specimens new and unusual to the States. During the latter years of her life, she also steadily expanded her horticultural pursuits and land holdings. At the time of her death in 1926, Arents owned eighty acres upon which she nurtured an inviting Victorian rose garden, specimen arboretum, and highly successful vegetable garden. Twentieth-century records indicate that people traveled great distances to study her agricultural practices. Today, several of Arents' trees continue to enhance the landscape of Lewis Ginter Botanical Garden, including the stately female ginkgo that has adorned the Bloemendaal side lawn for more than a century.

Richmond's Botanical Garden Is Born: Grace Arents had one final dream: to transform Bloemendaal Farm into a botanical garden. One year prior to her death, Arents penned the following will:

"I, Grace E. Arents of Bloemendaal Farm . . . being of sound and disposing mind and memory . . . do make and declare this to be my last will and testament . . . I do give, devise, and bequeath my farm in Henrico County, known as Bloemendaal Farm . . . to the City of Richmond . . . as a botanical garden . . . in perpetual memory of my Uncle Lewis Ginter to be known as the Lewis Ginter Botanical Garden. . . . This will is . . . signed by me this twenty-sixth day of July nineteen hundred and twenty-five." This bequest, along with a $100,000 endowment, provided the foundation for Lewis Ginter Botanical Garden, which first opened to the public in 1987 (*see* Historical Timeline).

Philanthropy and an appreciation for the importance of plants sparked the Garden's humble beginnings. Now, entering the twenty-first century, they continue to inspire the success, vitality, and fulfillment of Grace Arents' dream, which is realized through Lewis Ginter Botanical Garden.

Miss Grace Arents' rose garden, 1925

Historical Timeline 1880–1989

1894
Ginter built the Lakeside Wheel Club as a gathering place for bicycling enthusiasts.

1926
Grace Arents died at age seventy-eight; Arents willed life-rights of Bloemendaal residency to Mary Garland Smith, stipulating that following Smith's death the City of Richmond would develop the property as a botanical garden honoring Ginter.

1880 — 1890 — 1900 — 1910 — 1920 — 1930

1884
Lewis Ginter bought property in Richmond, Virginia, previously owned by Governor Patrick Henry and centuries earlier hunted by Powhatan Indians.

1897
Lewis Ginter died at age seventy-three from diabetes complications.

1896
Ginter opened Lakeside Park as another entertainment destination.

1917
Grace Arents converted Bloemendaal Farm into her private residence, since the founding of the Instructive Visiting Nurse Association ended the need for a children's convalescent home.

1913
Grace E. Arents, Ginter's niece, bought the Lakeside Wheel Club and property from Ginter's estate to create a convalescent home for sick children from the city who might benefit from the healthier, rural environment. She named it Bloemendaal Farm.

1968
Mary Garland Smith died at age 102; the City of Richmond acquired Bloemendaal Farm from Grace Arents' estate and used the property as a field nursery for the city parks.

1988
The Bloemendaal Society was founded as a volunteer organization; the first Visitors Center, The Shop in the Garden, and Library opened in the Bloemendaal House.

1987
Lewis Ginter Botanical Garden opened to the public.

1940   1950   1960   1970   1980   1990

1981
A committed group of botanists, horticulturists, and interested citizens formed Lewis Ginter Botanical Garden, Inc. to uphold Arents' will and initiated a lawsuit to create the Botanical Garden.

1984
An amicable settlement with the City of Richmond allowed the chartering of Lewis Ginter Botanical Garden; Robert S. Hebb was named the first executive director.

1984–1987
Bloemendaal House was restored; the first Master Plan was developed; and the first staff was hired.

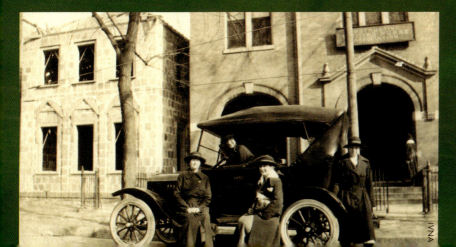

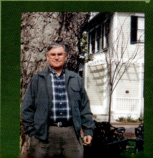

Historical Timeline
1990—2009

1991
Garland S. Sydnor Jr. served as the interim executive director; the Central Lake (now called Sydnor Lake) was funded by the Department of Historic Resources.

1993
Henry M. Flagler Perennial Garden and Asian Valley were dedicated; Lora and E. Claiborne Robins Tea House began dining service.

1996
Asian Valley was completed; Margaret Johanna Streb Conifer Garden opened.

1997
"A Growing Vision" $27-million capital campaign was announced.

1999
E. Claiborne Robins Visitors Center opened.

1990   *1999*

1990
The Grace E. Arents Garden was restored and dedicated by the Garden Club of Virginia; the Garden purchased additional land, increasing the property to eighty-two acres.

1992
Frank Robinson was named the second executive director.

1994
West Island Garden, Lucy Payne Minor Garden, and the Cottage Garden were completed; Bloemendaal House was redecorated.

1995
A revised Master Plan was presented by Higgins and Associates, Richmond, Virginia; first Children's Garden opened; first GardenFest of Lights.

1998
Asian Valley was expanded; Anne Holt Massey Greenhouses were completed.

2001
First Rose Garden and Belvedere were completed; Central Garden was completed.

2005
Children's Garden opened with vastly expanded offerings.

2009
Lewis Ginter Botanical Garden celebrated twenty-fifth anniversary.

2008
Rose Garden, Belvedere, and Terrace Lawn were expanded and dedicated.

2000 — *2009*

2003
Conservatory opened with its classically domed conservatory.

2002
Education and Library Complex opened.

2007
Sydnor Lake was dedicated.

2006
Garden Shop expanded; "A Growing Vision" capital campaign ended with contributions totaling $42 million.

THE GARDEN'S FUTURE
The Next Decade
BY FRANK ROBINSON, EXECUTIVE DIRECTOR

What does the future hold for Lewis Ginter Botanical Garden? The answer lies in its strategic plan, based on the Garden's vision, mission, and research related to our campus and the needs of our greater community. The strategic plan is a living document that will change with time and new opportunities, but as we see it in 2009, following are our priorities for continued growth.

Master Water Management Plan: We understand water is one of our most fundamental resources, and the Garden wants to serve as a model site in revealing how biological processes can and should be used to optimize the quality and management of surface and ground water. This is a multimillion-dollar project that will impact the entire Master Plan of the Garden. The outcome will be a teaching campus of regenerative design to demonstrate how the homeowner, corporate campus, public park, or large farm can be pro-active in preserving and maintaining our precious fresh water supply. In turn, the results will have beneficial impact on the James River and the Chesapeake Bay. This is an exciting opportunity that will take Lewis Ginter Botanical Garden to a new level of leadership in the nation. The water management plan includes the addition of major new gardens and two lakes as part of the regenerative design.

Children's Garden: Education through hands-on discovery and playful exploration within nature will remain the focus of Children's Garden future enhancements. Additional programs will be offered

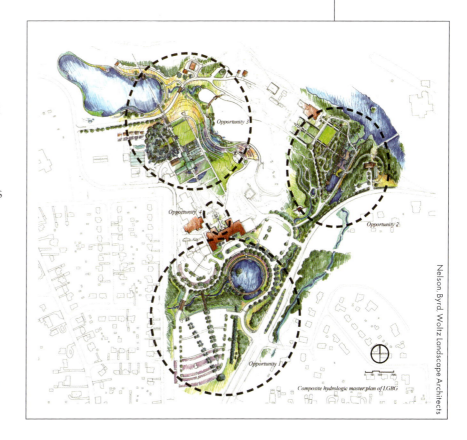

Proposed water management plan

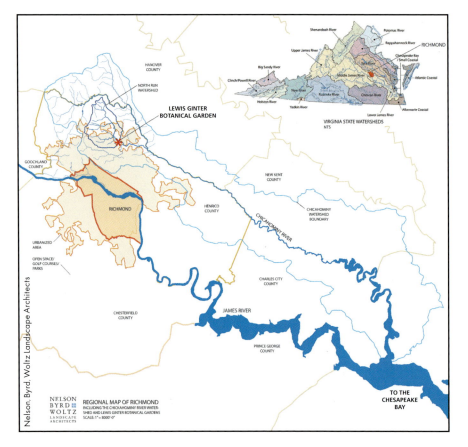

at the Garden and throughout the community. Expansion of classroom space and children's library facilities within a new LEED-certified "green" family education center will provide expanded year-round capacity for families, students, and educators.

Signature Gardens and Collections: As with the Children's Garden and the Rose Garden, Lewis Ginter wants to intentionally plan and refine its gardens and displays for outstanding quality. We will explore ways to enhance our current gardens, collections, and facilities, and will direct future resources to create a visitor experience which is unmatched anywhere in terms of aesthetics, education, and inspiration!

Sydnor Lake Enhancements: Along an axis that originates in the Central Garden and passes through the Terraced Lawn and Rose Garden, a dynamic illuminated water jet will rise from Sydnor Lake, creating an extraordinary experience of sight and sound. A 150-foot-long Promenade Bridge will provide a direct link between the Rose Garden and two ever-popular destinations: the Children's Garden and the Bloemendaal House. The bridge will gently curve along the shore of the West Island Garden, providing a dramatic platform to enjoy views across the water, day and night, as well as creating opportunities to enjoy both flora and fauna at close range.

Interpretation and Programs: One of the most challenging initiatives for any garden is to tell its stories—because there are so many to tell, and the plants can't talk. In additional to expanded signage, the garden will explore the opportunities provided by technology to interpret the significance of our collections and designed landscapes, the human stories behind the plants, the ways in which we can answer your questions and pique your curiosity, and how we can best disseminate the tremendous amount of useful information accumulated within our already substantial resources. We will also explore the ways in which we carry our fundamental messages into the broader community about the importance of nature to our very survival, as well as being mindful of optimizing our resources, and ensuring the most meaningful impact of our efforts.

VOLUNTEERISM

The Garden's volunteer corps is an integral part of its daily operation and service. Garden volunteers represent all ages, all walks of life, and all levels of skills and interest—yet they share two things in common—they love Lewis Ginter Botanical Garden and they merit deep appreciation from the Board of Directors and staff. Our volunteers serve in every capacity within the greater garden, from hands-on gardening to design projects for our holiday GardenFest of Lights. Our volunteer coordinator will be delighted to find a need to perfectly match your skills.

History: The Garden's history recounts the stories, talents, skills, and contributions of scores of community volunteers. Loyal supporters were first organized in 1988 as the Bloemendaal Society by founders Mary Mitchell, Polly Anderson, Joyce Sydnor, and Debbie Brooks. A Garden newsletter reported that 44 volunteers provided 800 hours of service that year. Less than two decades later, those numbers swelled to 462 volunteers whose 29,218 hours of service were valued at $289,000 in 2007 alone. Clearly, the Garden's success—now and in the future—is rooted in its volunteers.

MEMBERSHIP

The Garden's phenomenal growth also relies on its loyal membership, which today exceeds twelve thousand households, eight hundred patrons, and forty-five business members. Reasons for joining are as varied as the benefits: free admission to the Garden; special rates on ticketed and member-only events; discounts on education programs and Garden Shop purchases; seasonal editions of the *Garden Times;* and a shared commitment to the Garden's Mission.

Garden for All Seasons
SOMETHING NEW EVERY VISIT

The variance of seasons, succession of blooming, maturing of plantings, and fluctuating cycles of sunlight continually transform the Garden into an ever-changing feast for the senses. The visitor experience is enhanced by dramatic displays and family activities, educational programming and group tours, and special visitor amenities that range from shopping to dining.

Spring: As spring makes its presence known, nature beckons us to the great outdoors. This time of year, the Garden renews its glory, gradually greening and gracing its landscapes with rainbows of color and awesome beauty. Visitors of all ages respond in their own fashion, demonstrating a million ways to celebrate the season of **A Million Blooms**.

Summer: Take a leisurely, twilight garden stroll; try your hand at photography or birding; listen for the delights of childhood play; bring the family for a special event; wine and dine *al fresco*; or simply relax in quiet places. Summer is the season of glorious gardens and endless enjoyment.

Autumn: As the leaves turn, the Garden flaunts nature's multicolored splendor. Autumnal leaves enliven the landscape with blazes of color, while late-season flowers and ornamental grasses sway in the cool breeze, providing a fascinating segue to winter.

Winter: The inherent beauty of trees, shrubs, and landscapes is most apparent when shed of their leafy green façade. A stroll down frosty garden paths reveals not colorful blooms, but rather intrinsic shapes, gnarled trunks, interwoven branches, and delicate evergreen boughs. Winter encourages the visitor to see the garden with fresh eyes—a renewed awareness that recognizes and revels in nature's barren beauty.

Lewis Ginter Botanical Garden: 25 YEARS AND GROWING

Lewis Ginter Botanical Garden: 25 YEARS AND GROWING

An enchanting, festive glow also brightens the evening sky during the **GardenFest of Lights** holiday event. More than a half-million lights illuminate pathways, ponds, plants, and trees, as well as larger-than-life flowers, fairies, and fanciful figures. Since its 1992 premiere, GardenFest has become a community tradition that now entertains more than fifty-seven thousand visitors each year.

Lewis Ginter Botanical Garden: 25 YEARS AND GROWING

DESIGN TEAMS

The Board of Directors and staff of Lewis Ginter Botanical Garden played active roles in the conceptualization and planning of the Garden and facilities. The following provided professional expertise to bring those to fulfillment.

Project	Designer	Design Firm	Location	Construction	Location
1987 Master Plan	Jeffrey Rausch, Landscape Architect	Environmental Planning and Design	Pittsburgh, PA		
	Frederick Cox, Architect	Marcellus, Wright, Cox and Smith	Richmond, VA		
	Robert Hebb, Executive Director	Lewis Ginter Botanical Garden	Richmond, VA		
1995 Master Plan	Ralph Higgins, Landscape Architect	Higgins and Associates	Richmond, VA		
	Rodney Robinson, Allan Summers, Landscape Architects	RRLA Inc.	Wilmington, DE		
	Frank Robinson, Executive Director	Lewis Ginter Botanical Garden	Richmond, VA		
E. Claiborne Robins Visitors Center	Jacquelin T. Robertson	Cooper-Robertson	New York, NY	W. M. Jordan and Company	Newport News, VA
	Randy Holmes	The Glave Firm	Richmond, VA		
Central Garden	Rodney Robinson, Allan Summers	RRLA Inc.	Wilmington, DE	W. M. Jordan and Company	Newport News, VA
Education and Library Complex	Randy Holmes, Madge Bemiss	Glave and Holmes Associates	Richmond, VA	Kjellstrom and Lee, Inc.	Richmond, VA
Evelyn G. Luck Garden	Charles J. Stick	Charles J. Stick Inc.	Charlottesville, VA	Southern Brick	Richmond, VA
Conservatory	Madge Bemiss	Glave and Holmes Associates	Richmond, VA	Kjellstrom and Lee, Inc.	Richmond, VA
	Jim Smith	Rough Brothers	Cincinnati, OH		

Project	Designer	Design Firm	Location	Construction	Location
Rose Garden 2001	Rodney Robinson, Allan Summers	RRLA Inc.	Wilmington, DE	Kjellstrom and Lee, Inc.	Richmond, VA
Rose Garden 2008	Craig Reichbauer	Higgins and Gerstenmaier PLC	Richmond, VA	Hourigan Construction Corporation	Richmond, VA
Henry M. Flagler Garden	Jeffrey Rausch	Environmental Planning and Design	Pittsburgh, PA	Conquest, Moncure and Dunn	Richmond, VA
	Ian Robertson, Planting Plan	Ian Robertson, Ltd.	Charlottesville, VA		
Asian Valley Garden	Osamu Shimizu	Shimizu Landscape Design	Glen Echo, MD	Shimizu Landscape Design	Glen Echo, MD
Tea House	Jim Irby	Irby and Associates	Richmond, VA	Hayward and Lee	Richmond, VA
West Island Garden	Ian Robertson	Ian Robertson, Ltd.	Charlottesville, VA	In house	
Grace Arents Garden	Rudy J. Favretti	R. J. Favretti Landscape Architect	Storrs, CT		
Children's Garden	Herb Schaal	EDAW	Fort Collins, CO	Kjellstrom and Lee, Inc.	Richmond, VA
	Lewis Ginter Botanical Garden Staff	Lewis Ginter Botantical Garden	Richmond, VA		
		Forever Young Treehouses	Burlington, VT		
Sydnor Lake	Garland S. Sydnor	Sydnor Hydrodynamics	Richmond, VA	Lehigh Paving	Richmond, VA
Margaret Streb Garden	Ian Robertson	Ian Robertson, Ltd.	Charlottesville, VA	In house	
Lucy Payne Minor Garden	Ian Robertson	Ian Robertson, Ltd.	Charlottesville, VA	In house	
Anne Holt Massey Greenhouses	Randy Holmes	The Glave Firm	Richmond, VA	Prins Enterprises, Inc.	Fredericksburg, VA

BOARD OF DIRECTORS
1984–2008

The following individuals provided leadership through service on the Garden's Board of Directors:

A. Marshall Acuff Jr.
Eric C. Anderson
Judy Anderson
Susan H. Armstrong
Mae D. Augustine
Marvin Bagwell
D. Michael Baker
Robin Baliles
Jeannie Baliles
Dennis I. Belcher
Walton Belle
Elsie C. Bemiss
Elizabeth Bickel
Roger L. Boeve
Margaret Bowles
McEva R. Bowser
Charles Brown
Dr. Lucille M. Brown
Elisabeth Bryan
Childs F. Burden
Michele K. Burke
Al Caiazzo
Elizabeth Carr
Tazwell M. Carrington III
Herman L. Carter Jr.
Dr. Herbert A. Claiborne Jr.
Louis R. Clark
Katherine Clarke
Margaret Clement
Phyllis Cothran
Judson W. Collier Sr.
George T. Conwell
Frederic H. Cox Jr.
William Daniel
Courtnay Daniels
Michelle Duckett-Hedgebeth
C. Ross Edmonds Jr.
Beatrice Evans
S. Douglas Fleet
Charles H. Foster Jr.
Paul Funkhouser
Elizabeth Gardner
T. Fleetwood Garner
J. Samuel Gillespie Jr.
Barbara Glenn
The Honorable Richard W. Glover
Ellen M. Goodpasture
Ann Parker Gottwald
Nancy Gottwald
Barbara Grey
Robert J. Grey Jr., Esquire
Alex Grossman
Henry H. Harrell
Robert T. Haskins
Robert V. Hatcher Jr.
Florence B. Henderson
Ken Higgins
Richard G. Holder
Elizabeth Hughes
Velma P. Jackson
Jerry W. Jenkins
John Jennings
Warner M. Jones Sr.
Carolyn K. Keene, Ph.D.
Donna Kelliher
Karen E. Kelly
William H. King
Philip W. Klaus Jr.
Nathalie Klaus
The Honorable John Wingo Knowles
Rose Chen Lai
Lillian Lambert
Patricia Leggett
Janet Lewis
Lawrence Lewis
William Lohmann
Douglas Martin
Sally Maser
Joan Massey
Anne Holt Massey
Reverend Edward D. McCreary Jr.
Colette McEachin
Carroll J. McKenney
Lawrence McKoy
Brenda Mead
Katherine T. Mears
Lewis N. Miller Jr.
Mary Mitchell
J. Robert Mooney
Martha Moore
Helen Murphy
Robert Murphy
Rosalie Nachman
Curry Nelms
Neilson J. November
Richard W. Owen
William G. Pannill
Ellen Penick
Anthony R. D. Perrins
Edwina Phillips
Helen Pinckney
Fredrick G. Pollard
Roger A. Pond
Kenneth E. Powell
Robert H. Pratt
Carol Price
Ann Ramsey
John M. R. Reed
Charles L. Reed Jr.
Mary Lou Reinhart
Marietta Reynolds
Timothy D. Rhea
Deborah Roach
Doris H. Roberts
Lora M. Robins
Martha Robertson
A. Prescott Rowe
Elizabeth Saunders
Susan Scott
Charles H. Seilheimer Jr.
Jennie Shaw
David Shannon
Martha Sherman
Sandra Shield
Carolyn Snow
Jane Bassett Spilman
James H. Starkey III
Edward H. Starr Jr.
Donald A. Steinbrugge
Carolyn Stettinius
Jacquelyn E. Stone, Esquire
Jacque B. Sullivan
Garland S. Sydnor

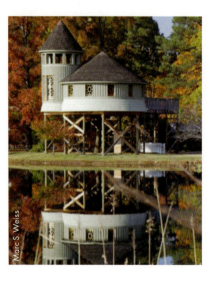

Raymond P. Szabo
Barbara Thalhimer
The Honorable John Charles Thomas
Mary Thompson
Matthew G. Thompson
Susan Thompson
Tim Timberlake
Peter C. Toms
H. Carlton Townes
Anthony F. Troy, Esquire
Ruby G. Turner
Katie Ukrop
Andre Viette
Kevin W. Walsh
Francis M. Watson
Clinton Webb
McDonald Wellford Jr.
Martha C. West
B. Briscoe White III
Ralph R. White Jr.
Mary Wick
Therese Wilson

C. J. O. Wodehouse Jr.
Deborah Wolenberg
Dr. Charlotte Woodfin
Elizabeth York

STAFF

The following staff members provided fifteen or more years of service during the Garden's first twenty-five years:

Susan Auburn
Erma Bouton
John Bouton
Peggy Combs
Martha Anne Ellis
Catherine Ellyson
Freda Lushbaugh
Joyce Paschall
Valerie Pascal
Kelly Riley
Frank Robinson

VOLUNTEERS

The following are Garden volunteers (as of year-end 2007) who generously contributed one thousand or more lifetime volunteer hours:

Dick Abbott
Julie Abbott
Polly Anderson
Mary Atkinson
Lynn Baldacci
Mabel Baldwin
Brenda Bartges
Sally Bingley
Martha Black
Lenny Blackwood
Brenda Boatwright
Dorothy Bruno
Helen Bunch
Dick Burch
Pat Chen
Roland Clement
Floyd Cox
Patricia Crone
Stanley Davis
Rex Dazey
Maya Debrunner
Dick Elcock
Virginia Fackler
Charles Fleming
Sharon Francisco
Carol Gill
Dean Goplerud
Suzanne Grasberger
Luella Hall
Ellen Hartenberg
Jane Hartough
Tom Hephner
Shirley Hughson

William Lacker
Virginia Love
Roberta Martin
Linda Miller
Kay Moore
Pat Moore
David North
Maggie North
Fran Purdum
Pres Purdum
Ann Reed
Stanley Reed Jr.
Mary Ann Rice
Tom Riddle
Hugh Rooney
E. K. Rose
Betsy Schrage
Dick Seltzer
Harriet Shaffer
Betsy Slade
Jody Smith
William Smith
Charlotte Trow
Jessie Turner
Bob Van Divender
Betty Walker
Bob Will
Marlu Winalski
Bee Wright

ACKNOWLEDGMENTS

Historical information for this publication was gleaned from the Garden's staff and archives; *Lewis Ginter Botanical Garden: A Short History* by Catherine Ellyson (1999); *A History of Bloemendaal* by Mary H. Mitchell and Robert S. Hebb (1986); and *Lewis Ginter, A Quiet Contribution* video by County of Henrico (2008).

Historical images were supplied by The Valentine Richmond History Center, the Instructive Visiting Nurse Association, and the County of Henrico. Current images were shared by visitors, staff, and professionals who captured the Garden's beauty through their talented photography.

ABOUT THE EDITOR

Frank L. Robinson has served as Lewis Ginter Botanical Garden's executive director since 1992. During Robinson's seventeen-year tenure, his horticultural experience, leadership, and vision—coupled with strong staff, board, and donor support—have transformed the Garden from a local destination to a regional attraction for visitors of all ages.

ABOUT THE AUTHOR

Lynn J. Kirk, freelance writer and public relations consultant, has written on behalf of Lewis Ginter Botanical Garden since 2004. In addition to this anniversary publication, she serves as editor for the *Garden Times* newsletter and co-authors a monthly gardening column for the *Richmond Times-Dispatch*.